BRITAIN IN PICTURES
THE BRITISH PEOPLE IN PICTURES

BRITISH DRAMATISTS

105

D0101329

GENERAL EDITOR
W. J. TURNER

*

The Editor is most grateful to all those who have
so kindly helped in the selection of illustrations,
especially to officials of the various public
Museums, Libraries and Galleries, and
to all others who have generously
allowed pictures and MSS.
to be reproduced.

BRITISH DRAMATISTS

GRAHAM GREENE

---

*WITH
8 PLATES IN COLOUR
AND
26 ILLUSTRATIONS IN
BLACK & WHITE*

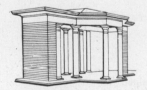

WILLIAM COLLINS OF LONDON
MCMXXXXII

PRODUCED BY
ADPRINT LIMITED LONDON

✳

PRINTED
IN GREAT BRITAIN
BY WILLIAM BROWN AND CO. LTD. LONDON

PR628
67

LIST OF ILLUSTRATIONS

PLATES IN COLOUR

BLACK AND WHITE ILLUSTRATIONS

904173

BLACK AND WHITE ILLUSTRATIONS

ANYONE WHO GOES INTO A ROMAN CATHOLIC CHURCH during the Holy Week services, can see for himself the origin of our drama : on Palm Sunday the priest knocks on the door of the church and demands to be admitted, the palms are borne along the aisle : on Good Friday the shrill voices of Judas and the High Priest break into the narrative of the Gospel : the progress to Calvary is made more real by human actors.

It seems a long road to have travelled—from this to the drunken ladies of Noel Coward's *Private Lives*, and one which can only lightly be sketched in so short a book as this. But there remains all the time—whether we are considering the latest Drayton-Hare farce or the enormous despair of *King Lear*—the sense of ritual. Perhaps the child is more aware of it than the grown man at the theatre : the chatter subdued as the overture begins, or else the three sudden raps like those of the priest at the church door : the regular rise and fall of the curtain between our world and theirs. To the child it little matters what happens upon the stage : the ritual is there—the magic : the maid who crosses the stage towards the ringing telephone as the curtain goes up has to the innocent eye the appearance of an acolyte moving from left to right before the altar.

Even though little evidence is available for the years between it is easy enough to conjecture the way in which the drama began. On one side of the narrow gap is the Mass with its dramatic re-enactment of the Last Supper : on the other the Mystery and Miracle Plays—incidents from the Old and the New Testaments, legends of saints acted often by priests, in the precincts of churches. Popularity drove these plays out of the church into the churchyard where the feet of the mob trampled over the graves. And so to save the graves they had to go further and become more secularised. Acted at fairs on movable scaffolds, forming part of the riotous medieval processions, played by jugglers and members of trade guilds, their subject-matter widened. Noah could be drunk in a market-place as he could not be in a church. And so when we look again towards the end of the

7

fifteenth century we find the drama flourishing in nearly a hundred towns, religious still but sometimes twisting into odd Gothic humours. Four great cycles of Miracle Plays (known as the York, Towneley, Chester and Coventry) are still in existence, representing the whole biblical story from the Creation to the Ascension. Of the York cycle we have the order of the Pageant on Corpus Christi, 1415, with each guild assigned its part in the gigantic cycle of the Fall and the Redemption : the Tanners, the Plasterers, Cardmakers, Fitters, Coopers and Armourers, Glovers, Shipwrights, Fishmongers, Bookbinders, Hosiers, Spicers and Pewterers and Chandlers and Vintners — the list is only limited by man's needs. These plays grew, like a church, anonymously : we have reached the drama, but not yet the dramatist.

One reads these plays now for pedantry rather than for pleasure ; where humour or a kind of simple poetry creeps in, perhaps we value it too highly for the contrast : the scene in the Chester play of *Noah's Flood* when Noah's wife refuses to enter the ark :—

> " Yea, sir, sette up youer saile,
> And rowe fourth with evill haile,
> For withouten anye faiyle
>   I will not oute of this towne ;
> But I have my gossippes everichone,
> One foote further I will not gone :
> They shall not drowne, by Sante John !
> And I may save their life."

the scene in *The Sacrifice of Isaac* when Abraham prepares to kill his " sweet sonne of grace " ; or most striking of all—like a comic gargoyle on a Cathedral roof—the *Secunda Pastorum* in the Towneley Plays when just before the Angels sing their *Gloria in Excelsis* we watch the shepherds search the house of Mak, the sheepstealer, and at last find the missing ewe wrapped in swaddling clothes — a bold caricature—lying in a cradle.

> " Gyf me lefe hym to kys, and lyft up the clowtt.
> What the deville is this ? he has a long snowte."

Alongside the Miracle Play grew up the Morality, of which the story was only the vehicle to illustrate the beauty of virtue and the ugliness of vice. This is the abstract theme of later drama robbed of the particular plot and particular characters—Macbeth appears only as Ambition and Iago as Deceit. It is the bones without the flesh, just as so often in twentieth century drama we have the flesh without the bones—characters who act a plot before us and have no significance at all outside the theatre, who are born when the curtain rises and die when it falls.

The Morality play reached its highest point with *Everyman*, composed before the end of the 15th century, a play of such permanent interest that it excludes

By courtesy of the Garrick Club, London

A SCENE FROM *VENICE PRESERVED* : A TRAGEDY BY THOMAS OTWAY

David Garrick as " Jaffier " and Mrs. Cibber as " Belvidera "

Oil painting by John Zoffany

By courtesy of the Trustees of the National Portrait Gallery, London

JOHN DRYDEN 1631–1700
Oil painting by James Maubert

from the attention of all but scholars its predecessors and contemporaries, just as the ordinary man's knowledge of Elizabethan drama is justifiably confined almost entirely to Shakespeare's plays. That it is founded on an original Dutch version is neither here nor there : it lives as poetry and the poetry is English. The plot is as bone-dry and unadorned as the verse : it belongs to the world of the Black Death and the theological argument. God sends Death to Everyman to summon him to judgment, and Everyman's cry, " O Death, thou comest when I had thee least in mynde ", bare and precise and human, goes echoing through the century which separates him from Shakespeare to reappear in the more studied, more evocative, but hardly more telling Renaissance cry : " She should have died hereafter. There would have been a time for such a word "—all that fear of death's heavy responsibility which belongs to the Age of Faith and lay on Hamlet's will as much as Everyman's. Everyman tries in vain to bribe Death to delay : but Death is unbribable. He tries to wring out some hope of return. All he can procure is consent that he may take with him a friend on his journey.

And so Everyman goes first to Fellowship, and here under the abstract name we can see the dramatist beginning to evolve character—much as novelists of the 18th and 19th centuries hid a particular man under the abstract name— Mr. Allworthy, Sir Gregory Hardlines and the like. Bluff, cheerful, bogus Fellowship is not quite an abstraction as he greets Everyman : there is nothing he will not do for a friend : only let him name his grief : he will die for him : he will go to Hell for him, but the straight name of Death on his friend's lips freezes his promises.

> " Now, by God that all hathe bought,
> If deth were the messenger,
> For no man that is lyvynge todaye
> I will not go that lothe journaye,
> Not for the fader that bygote me."

There is no room to follow Everyman's course in detail : from Fellowship to Good Deeds :—

> " Here I lye, cold in the grounde,
> Thy synnes hath me sore bounde
> That I can not stire ; "

and on to Knowledge who leads him to Confession, and so to the last sacrament and his farewell to Beauty and Strength, Discretion and the Five Wits, all except Good Deeds. The pilgrimage is conventional, but it is passionately described : it is theologically exact, because that exactitude seemed to the fifteenth century author to express the truth. It is the first English play that belongs to our living literature, and we have to wait nearly a hundred years for another.

In the interval something new emerges—the author.

THESE first authors are not of great interest except historically, and that is because the theatre was still the fair and the market-place. To try to revive these plays in a different *milieu* would be like trying to revive on the great screen, before the huge auditorium of the modern cinema, some little reel of celluloid made for the nickelodeon. The theatre is a popular art, and we must not confuse the historical interest—confined to a few—with the dramatic interest. *Everyman* lives as poetry, and as a play, but these first experiments in secular drama, by men like Heywood and Bale, have not that much life in their dry bones : Folly, Hypocrisy, Good Deeds and the rest have been given names—they become Johan the Husband, Tyb the Wife, Sir Jhon the Priest, Neighbour Prattle. They have a rough humour, satire as blunt and heavy as a quarter-staff—that applies to Heywood. Bale introduced history—*Kynge Johan* and *Apius and Virginia*. It is the period of Henry and Mary, when religion is becoming confused with politics, and it is really safer to leave religion alone. Men who write plays have heads to lose and their bodies are as inflammable as others.

The New Learning too had arrived, and simple men, it may well be, were ceasing to write in these confusing times. The unknown authors of the early Miracles were not men of intelligence—they were men of feeling, and men who had been taught rather than teachers. The moralities are like children's lessons. The new plays are ceasing to be popular ; they are written at Eton for Etonians, acted in colleges and in the Inns of Court, with Terence and Seneca for models, and the stage has become at last stationary—but not in a market-place (though it must be remembered that the mob could still see the old Miracles and Moralities —they were being acted here and there as late as when Hamlet took the stage, just as the Morality, if you look for it, still lingers today at the seaside in the Punch booth).

The drama had become separated from the people, and it will not really interest us again until the audience has once more become popular. We are interested in the dramatists of these days only as stations along a line, and we have to go a long way before the line curves and returns towards the market where we started.

So Heywood and Bale are important only as the rude precursors of George Gascoyne and Sackville and Norton, who in turn are only important because they lead us a little nearer to the day when, without warning, the greatest playwright the world has known broke on his age. Sackville and Norton, whose monstrous *Gorboduc* (1562) was an exact imitation of Seneca, mark a stage because they were the first to use dramatic blank verse. This new way of writing, the freedom from rhyme, the approach to realism made possible by the broken rhythm, released the dramatic imagination : the speed with which the drama developed from this point is comparable to the speed with which the film developed. How astonishing

MAN SURROUNDED BY THE VIRTUES, RECEIVES THE MESSAGE FROM DEATH
Illumination from Thomas Chaundler's *Liber Apologeticus*

it is to think that Elizabeth, who listened one January night in 1562 to *Gorboduc* in the Inner Temple Hall, was able to listen forty years later to *Twelfth Night*. Hear the ghosts in that bombed, deserted hall intoning *Gorboduc* before the court :—

> " We then, alas, the ladies which that time
> Did there attend, seeing that heinous deed,
> And hearing him oft call the wretched name
> Of mother, and to cry to her for aid
> Whose direful hand gave him the mortal wound,
> Pitying—alas, (for nought else could we do),
> His ruthful end, ran to the woeful bed,
> Despoiled straight his breast, and all we might,
> Wiped in vain with napkins next at hand . . ."

The instrument had been invented, but who that night could have foretold these sounds from it?

> " O, fellow, come, the song we had last night.
> Mark it, Cesario, it is old and plain ;
> The spinsters and the knitters in the sun
> And the free maids that weave their thread with bones
> Do use to chant it : it is silly sooth,
> And dallies with the innocence of love,
> Like the old age."

You cannot simply say that Shakespeare was a poet, and that Sackville and Norton were not : the difference to an audience was less subtle than that. These lines of Shakespeare's are *realistic* : they refer to the common, known life, they have the uneven rhythm of speech and grammatically they are simple. How difficult by comparison are the involved periods of *Gorboduc*. The audience must often have found themselves hopelessly lost in the maze of those immense rhetorical sentences. They lie over the drama like the folds of a heavy toga impeding movement.

What filled those forty years? One is inclined to answer simply, Marlowe, but of course there were others, hammering at that stiff formal medium, increasing the subject-matter of verse. Religion was better left alone for the time (and afterwards found itself left alone for good) so that Shakespeare only allowed himself occasional glancing lines (Hamlet's prayer, the papal nuncio rebuking Philip of France) which showed just the fin of the dangerous thoughts moving below the surface. We are still dealing more with the history of verse than of the stage : Kyd, remembered by scholars for *The Spanish Tragedie*, in which the blank verse was constructed with euphemisms as complicated as the dingy plot, but where the play began to lose the bogus dignity of the pseudo-Seneca ; Robert Greene who would hardly be remembered today if he had not sneered at the young Shakespeare as an " upstart crow ", written a few songs which please anthologists, and drunk very deeply ; George Peele and Lyly—but they are too

INTERIOR OF THE SWAN THEATRE IN 1596
Contemporary drawing by John de Witt

many to notice here, these men whose plays only survive in the memory of scholars and enthusiasts. To Greene alone perhaps is this judgment a little unfair: Greene with his idealised milk maids, cool-fingered, spiritual and content, who ranged the air above the dreary room, the alehouse and the stews which formed his actual scene—a scene more pleasing to scholars than to men who live those lives. But even Greene belongs more to a record of minor poetry than to a record of drama.

THE GLOBE THEATRE, SOUTHWARK, C. 1612
Here most of Shakespeare's plays were performed between 1599-1613
Engraving from Wilkinson's *Theatrum Illustrata*

We are dealing in this book with dramatists and not with the mechanics of the stage : but it is essential to note in passing the changing *milieu* – from church-yard to market-place, from market-place to the great household where the peer could watch the players without smelling the vulgar, and from the peer's house-hold, with the support of their patron, into the inn yards. Then in 1576 came the blow which looked like attaching playwrights permanently to the household, when the Corporation of London forbade the performance of plays in public within the bounds for the sake of morality and hygiene. But this was answered in the same year with the first theatre, in Shoreditch, outside the city limits, and so for the first time we get the fixed stage, the management, the responsibility towards an audience, the profit-and-loss account – all those considerations which the dilettante regards as unseemly checks on the freedom of the artist, but which the artist knows to be the very mould of his technique and the challenge to his imagination. It is nothing to wonder at that it took less than thirty years then to produce *Hamlet*, but one may well speculate whether without the commercial theatre the dramatists would ever have risen higher than the learned imitations of Seneca or Terence, or the elaborate and poetic conceits of Lyly.

The result was not immediately seen – even Marlowe did not belong to *his* stage in the easy way that the miracle players belonged to theirs. Perhaps there

INSIDE THE RED BULL PLAYHOUSE, CLERKENWELL
Engraved frontispiece Kirkman's *Drolls*, 1672

is no dramatist more over-rated—and that because his plays are only read and seldom seen. Perhaps it would be wrong to say that *Tamburlaine* is as unactable as *Philip van Arteveld* because it has, in its day, been acted, but one detects no enthusiasm even in such classically-minded theatres as the Old Vic for trying the experiment again. Marlowe was a fine poet who can be seen at his best in his translations from Ovid: fine lustful realistic couplets which remind us of Donne's satires. Stray lines from *Dr. Faustus* and *Tamburlaine* have lodged in the popular memory: the general effect of his work is of a great gallery lit by the sun and lined with statues, hung with pictures, littered by valuable cabinets, tables, *objets d'art*, so many that they end in tedium: the vulgarity of renaissance riches, the over-enjoyment of life, and the concupiscence of a young man. He had immense potentialities which glimmer through the interminable boring rant of *Tamburlaine* and the broken-backed construction of *Dr. Faustus*: in *Edward II* he came nearer to writing a fine play in which the occasional poetry was conditioned by the action and held in check by character. But he meddled too much in active life: the speculations which brought him a fine for blasphemy were really safer: he was stabbed not, as we used to learn, by a tavern-roisterer, but—as Dr. Hotson discovered a few years ago—by a political spy, leaving behind him at the age of twenty-nine a few fine torsos, some mutilated marble. It is always idle to speculate about a dead man's future: a man dies in the way he lives—and Marlowe's life and talent were both spectacular.

He is a telling contrast to his great successor—whom even Greene had sneered at. This is the sort of life we need for great achievement: so anonymous that even rumour runs off the smooth flanks like water: the man who simply works day in, day out, part of the theatre like the boards worn by actors' feet, protectively covered, with no ambition known to his fellows but the one we all can share—of a house and land and security in troubled times. The rumours of unhappy marriage, of a dark mistress and homosexual love, carry the biographer nowhere; nobody who lives escapes a private agony: one can assume them in Shakespeare's case without, like a gossip-writer, fixing the wrong public name. The important thing is the plays, more important even than the poetry, for poetry alone cannot make a good play (or else Tennyson's *Queen Mary*, which contains some of the finest verse he wrote, would live upon the stage).

Obviously, the whole length of this book would be inadequate to deal with one of Shakespeare's plays; let us in the pitiably small space allowed consider this first and greatest Man of the Theatre without looking at the poet. He had, of course, to learn—as no one after him, until we come to the prose Restoration play, had to learn again: he did the work for all. If *Edward II* was the height his predecessors reached, that was little enough for him to build on. Consider these points: how a play begins, how it proceeds, and how it ends. What did *Edward II*

16

WILLIAM SHAKESPEARE
Engraving by Martin Droeshout
Frontispiece to the first folio edition of 1623

have to offer to the future then? A good plain opening, it may be said, with Gaveston reading a letter from the King recalling him to England; but from that point we proceed dryly and choppily by chronological stages—like *Little Arthur's History of England*—the meeting with the King, the quarrel with Coventry, the peer's anger, the banishment to Ireland, the recall again to England—all this compressed shapelessly into a single act which has no unity of itself, where no scene prepares you for the next, without the sense of destiny, the thread on which, rather than the passage of time, a play's scenes should be strung. And what is the play's end? After the horrifying murder of Edward—in which Marlowe's dramatic genius reached its height and the violence of his spirit found for once perfect expression—we have a sorry little hustled postscript in which the young prince— who has hardly been established as a character—turns on the Queen and Mortimer and avenges his father's death. We feel cheated—rather as when the murderer in a detective story proves to be someone who only appears in the last chapter. And

SCENE FROM *THE TAMING OF THE SHREW*
Engraving from the first illustrated edition of
Shakespeare, edited by Nicholas Rowe, 1709

how did Marlowe use the chief handicap and—in the right hands—the chief asset of the Elizabethan stage—the absence of scenery? Certainly he improved on *Gorboduc*, whose authors saw in this only an enforced and colourless unity. The scenes of *Tamburlaine*, unlimited by pasteboard sets and an expense-sheet, shifted boldly all over Asia : *Edward* moved here and there, to London and Warwickshire and Pontefract, but the shifts are never made visible to the audience. The only scene that writes itself on the inner eye is in the bare prison cell, the castle's sewer.

One disparages Marlowe only to throw up into greater relief the craftsmanship of Shakespeare : those first scenes which grip us like the Ancient Mariner's eye – the angry mutterings in the Venice streets, the sudden broil which brings Othello on the scene ("Put up your bright swords or the dew will rust them"): the witches loitering on the road to Forres ; the heroes returning from the field of Troy and passing under Cressida's balcony. The endings : Othello's "base Indian" lament : Cleopatra's death : the fool's ironical song at the end of *Twelfth Night* ; the violence of Hamlet and the sudden close— "the rest is silence"; the verbal power which continually puts a scene before our eyes far more vividly than the later scene-painters could do it : the dark after-midnight castle where Duncan lies : the forest of Arden : the battlements of Elsinore.

We confuse the issue when we talk of Shakespeare's greatness as a poet : in the plays the poetry is rightness—that is nearly all : the *exact* expression of a mental state : the *exact* description of a scene. "Think, we had mothers," Troilus's bitter outburst is not poetry in any usually accepted meaning of the word—it is simply the right phrase at the right moment, a mathematical accuracy as if this astonishing man could measure his words against our nature in a balance sensitive to the fraction of a milligramme. The effect it has on our minds is roughly similar to the effect of poetry, but the emphasis on the poetic content of the plays had a disastrous effect on the future— for it made poets think they were dramatists.

We have left out of account what the modern dramatist considers most important of all— character. Of course Shakespeare created characters— Falstaff, Macbeth, Cressida; but was Hamlet a character, or Lear, or Iago—any more than Marlowe's Faustus? They are mouthpieces for a mood, for an attitude to life, far more than characters, and it is doubtful whether in fact Shakespeare's plays depend on character at all. *Twelfth Night*, his most perfect

SCENE FROM *A MIDSUMMER NIGHT'S DREAM*
Engraving from the first illustrated edition of Shakespeare, edited by Nicholas Rowe 1709

play contains no character; Viola, Olivia, the Duke—they have just enough of our human nature to play their light lyrical parody of human emotion: Aguecheek and Sir Toby and Malvolio—these are fantasies not characters. In that lovely play all is surface. It must be remembered that we are still within the period of the Morality : they are being acted yet in the country districts : they had been absorbed by Shakespeare, just as much as he absorbed the plays of Marlowe, and the abstraction—the spirit of Revenge (Hamlet), of Jealousy (Othello), of Ambition (Macbeth), of Ingratitude (Lear), of Passion (Anthony and Cleopatra)—still rules the play. And rightly. Here is the watershed between the morality and the play of character : the tension between the two is perfectly kept: there is dialectical perfection. After Shakespeare, character—which was to have its dramatic triumphs—won a too-costly victory.

19

PERHAPS the most startling line of poetry in all our literature occurs in one of Shakespeare's sonnets : " Desiring this man's scope and that man's art." Whose scope could the man who wrote both *Twelfth Night* and *Troilus and Cressida* have envied, and whose art ? Perhaps the writer who had made poetry realistic envied the conceits of Lyly and Greene : perhaps the creator of Falstaff envied the stiff magnificent dignity of Jonson. We are tempted to the opposite extreme : to be aware only of silence after the burial in Stratford.

But that is unjust to Shakespeare. He had taught the craft of the theatre ; he had lifted the play on to a level which even without his genius was to remain higher than the one he had found. We have only to compare Jonson's *Sejanus* with the pre-Shakespearian historical plays to notice the difference. The play is less flexible than, say, *Julius Caesar*, dramatically and rhythmically, but what an advance it is on *Edward II*. The blank verse is a little stiff, but it is vivid with the sense of life observed from almost the first lines :—

> " We have no shift of faces, no cleft tongues,
> No soft and glutinous bodies, that can stick
> Like snails on painted walls . . ."

In this, Jonson's first play beyond the prentice stage, we notice the quality which reached its height in the great comedies — *Volpone* and *The Alchemist* — the concrete common image — a kind of man-in-the-street poetry :—

> " . . . which by asserting
> Hath more confirm'd us, than if heart'ning Jove
> Had, from his hundred statues, bid us strike,
> And at the stroke *click'd all his marble thumbs*."

An ex-bricklayer and a braggart who had fought in the Low Countries and killed his man in a duel, the tyrant of a literary group in a favourite inn, he was conscious of his art as no one but Shakespeare had been before him. He might have written Dryden's prefaces — except that his prose was not good enough : he did not believe in happy accidents or fine frenzies — Shakespeare seems all spirit beside his earthly sturdy talent. One admires the quality one lacks, and we know how Jonson admired Shakespeare, but Shakespeare may well have admired in Jonson the sense of huge enjoyment. The sensuality of Volpone or Sir Epicure Mammon is described by a man whom the world has treated well :—

> " I will have all my beds blown up, not stuft :
> Down is too hard : and then, mine oval room
> Fill'd with such pictures as Tiberius took
> From Elephantis, and dull Aretine
> But coldly imitated. Then, my glasses
> Cut in more subtle angles, to disperse
> And multiply the figures, as I walk
> Naked between my succubae . . ."

BEN JONSON, 1573(?)—1637
Panel after Gerard Honthorst

Compare this with those self-torturing lines out of *The Winter's Tale* (a comedy !):—

" . . . There have been,
Or I am much deceived, cuckolds e'er now ;
And many a man there is, even at this present,
Now while I speak this, holds his wife by th'arm,
That little thinks she has been sluiced in's absence,
And his pond fish't by his next neighbour, by
Sir Smile, his neighbour . . ."

" It is a bawdy planet, that will strike
Where 'tis predominant ; and 'tis powerful, think it,
From east, west, north and south ; be it concluded,
No barricado for a belly. . . ."

Even to Falstaff Shakespeare gave sombre thoughts, his streaks of pathos; none of Shakespeare's characters belongs to pure comedy—tragedy creeps in with Shylock, with the ageing Falstaff, with a fool's song : heart-break is always near while " the worm feeds on the damask cheek " ; but the fate of Volpone does not worry us ; Jonson alone has presented on the stage the full rich enjoyment of life —this is his real achievement, not his theory of " humours " which the professors discuss at such length and which he himself considered so important. His range is narrow : nearly all his comedies—and all his best—turn on the humour of the gull and the astute rogue ; his verse has not the speed, the vigour, the irregularity of Shakespeare, but he remains the greatest reporter of his age.

THE Elizabethan is usually regarded as the richest period of our drama, but it is the Jacobean which saw the greatest plays : the best of Shakespeare and Ben Jonson. Even the minor playwrights had learned the lesson of the master, and none of the smaller Elizabethan fry reached the level of Webster, Massinger, Beaumont and Fletcher, Chapman, even Ford and Tourneur.

There is no space in a book of this size to deal at any length with these authors individually. There was the difficult metaphysical treatment of melodrama which makes Chapman, the author of the two plays of *Bussy D'Ambois* and *The Duke of Biron*, more interesting for the study than the stage, where clarity, directness, speed are necessary ; even in his own life, when the taste of the audience was so infinitely superior to that of our own day, he was a failure and could have written with more justice and quite as much pride as Jonson :—

> " Make not thyself a Page
>   To that Strumpet the Stage,
>   But sing high and aloofe,
>   Safe from the Wolves black Jaw, and the dull Asses Hoofe."

Far more successful with the Jacobean audience were the romantic pair, Beaumont and Fletcher, who handed on the theme of Honour to Dryden and the Restoration tragedians in plays packed to absurdity with scruples ; even the best, *The Maid's Tragedy*, contains situations as grotesquely unreal as when Aspasia dresses in boy's clothes and incites her faithless lover to a duel so that she may die by his hands. Yet the plays are saved by a youthful lyricism as fresh as the Elizabethan and less conceited, with a charming sensuous sexuality which makes the marriage preparations in *The Maid's Tragedy* as free from offence as Spenser's *Epithalamium*. Of all these dramatists Webster stands alone by virtue of his one great play, *The Duchess of Malfi*, the only play of which it is possible to say that, owing

ILLUSTRATION TO THE DRAMATIC WORKS OF BEAUMONT AND FLETCHER
Water colour by Michael Rooker, 1743-1801

nothing to Shakespeare, it yet stands on a level with the great tragedies. *The White Devil* had showed him to be a poet of some erratic genius : it would have left a memory of morbid and magnificent lines : we should have remembered him with Ford and Tourneur, a group who share a kind of dark horror, a violent moral anarchy which seems to have followed the Elizabethan age like a headache after a feast. Among these writers you are aware of no moral centre, no standard of moral criticism — your hero may be an incestuous murderer, the most moving lines may be put in the mouth of an adulteress who has plotted the murder of her husband. In

King Lear the cruelty of the world may appal us, but somewhere outside there is virtue : the seventeenth century is not eternity, and death is an escape and not an end. But in Tourneur and the earlier Webster we are in the company of men who would really seem to have been lost in the dark night of the soul if they had had enough religious sense to feel despair : the world is all there is, and the world is violent, mad, miserable and without point. The religious revolution had had its effect : this was the rough uneasy straits which led to the serene Anglicanism of Herbert and Vaughan, and to the sceptical doldrums of the eighteenth century : in between the old unquestioning faith and the new toleration lay an unhappy atheism, which has none of the youthful rebelliousness of Marlowe's :—

> " We are merely the stars' tennis balls, struck and bandied
> Which way please them."

That attitude carried to Tourneur's extreme cannot make a good play, though it can make great poetry. Put on the lowest grounds—an audience must know whom to clap and whom to hiss. Webster's Vittoria Corombona, conceived as a devil, is transformed by the poetry of the trial scene into a heroine—it is too confusing.

But Webster emerged. Bosolo, the self-tortured tool of the Duchess of Malfi's brothers, has the bitter voice of an exile who has not quite forgotten. In his despair he uses heavenly images :—

> " What's this flesh? a little crudded milk, fantastical puff paste. Our bodies are weaker than those paper prisons boys use to keep flies in ; more contemptible, since ours is to preserve earthworms. Didst thou ever see a lark in a cage? Such is the soul in the body : this world is like her little turf of grass, and the Heav'n o'er our heads, like her looking glass, only gives us a miserable knowledge of the small compass of our prison."

An exile who has not quite forgotten, a prisoner who knows by his own fate that there is such a thing as liberty—that is why Webster is an incomparably finer dramatist than Tourneur. He emerges in his later play far enough from the darkened intellectual world to organise—Vittoria Corrombona speaks with the voice of angels, but the Duchess of Malfi is on the side of the angels. And on the side, too, of ordinary commonplace humanity. Nowhere among this group of dramatists—except fleetingly in Ford—will you find the note of recognisable everyday tenderness as you find it in Webster, in the love scene when the Duchess gently forces Antonio to declare his love. It is as if the dark Jacobean vapours are lifting, and almost anything might have been expected of Webster if he had not died. Alone of these men he left behind something essentially his : only a scholar could differentiate between untitled scraps of the other poets, but Webster's tone is unmistakable—the keen, economical, pointed oddity of the dialogue—whether in prose or verse—expressing the night side of life :—

By courtesy of the Trustees of the National Portrait Gallery, London

WILLIAM CONGREVE 1670–1729
Oil painting by Sir Godfrey Kneller

By courtesy of the Trustees of the National Portrait Gallery, London

OLIVER GOLDSMITH 1728–1774
Oil painting ; studio of Sir Joshua Reynolds

> " How tedious is a guilty conscience.
> When I look into the fishpond in my garden,
> Methinks I see a thing armed with a rake
> That seems to strike at me."

In this one respect his power was greater than Shakespeare's. That enormous genius must be allowed his limitations ; even in his darkest period he was too sane, too conscious of his art, to express madness convincingly. The mad Lear is no more mad than Hamlet—he is only distraught, and Ophelia and her flowers is a pretty conceit that might have come from one of Greene's novels. Surrealism is an overworked and a dubious term, but an intellectual generation which has rediscovered Blake and wandered with Dedalus and Bloom through the Dublin night should be quick to recognise the quality of Webster :—

> " Woe to the caroche that brought home my wife from the masque at three o'clock in the morning ! It had a large feather bed in it."

The astonishing thing is not that Webster has so small a public to-day but that he once had so large a one, the great popular audiences of the playhouse—this was what going to the play meant then that to-day means watching a Van Druten, a St. John Ervine or a Dodie Smith.

THE enormous tide ebbed, and it was nearly fifty years before the English theatre produced another man of genius ; a few names are left on the beach for scholars to pore over—Shirley, known to everyone for his lyric, " The Glories of our Blood and State, " from *Ajax and Ulysses*; Suckling, whose *Ballad of a Wedding* is worth all his tedious blank verse plays ; and Sir William Davenant, a fine lyric writer but an indifferent playwright, though he claimed to be Shakespeare's bastard (is the story too well known to repeat here of the priest who met the child Davenant running up Oxford High Street towards the Turl where he lived, and asked him what was the hurry? He replied that his godfather Shakespeare had come, to which the priest replied, " Why do you take the name of God in vain ? " The tale is Davenant's own).

The moon which drew the tide back was civil war, the triumph of the Puritans. The theatres had always had a precarious existence : now they stopped altogether. The Puritan spirit ruled the country as much as the town : there were no longer any bounds beyond which the theatre could migrate : the market place as a centre of enjoyment had ceased to exist and the day of the miracle play was at last done. Men began to write plays to be read only : the literary quality of dialogue became more important than the dramatic : life was extinguished between calf boards.

It is wrong to think of the years of the Civil War and the Protectorate as an interlude merely between two dramatic periods—the closing of the theatres had as permanent an effect on our literature as the beheading of a king had on our constitution. The theatre had begun by being popular, had become a " class " entertainment and then become popular again ; now it ceased to be anything but the recreation of the educated, the aristocratic, and later, when these two terms ceased to be synonymous, of the well-to-do. The people were to disappear—or to become a few rude voices from the gallery reported in the Press with disapproval after a First Night. Most of us have been present on some occasion of baffled dislike among the " Gods "—a courtesy title like that given to Prime Ministers after the power has gone : the hisses and catcalls from the gallery are drowned by the claps from the stalls, who feel that the author in some mysterious way belongs to them.

And belong he does. The Puritans saw to that. Shakespeare had belonged to the people, catching for the first time in verse the accent of common speech, giving them the violent, universal tragedies they understood—Doll Tearsheet and the murderer's knife and the laughter of clowns, and of course so much more : Jonson, too, had belonged to them, with his broad realism and downright poetry. They had served the people and the people had moulded them. The frequenters of bear-baiting demanded vitality : men and women who had watched from their windows the awful ritual of the scaffold were ready for any depth of horror the playwright cared to measure.

But when the play returned, it returned almost literally to the drawing-room. There are always ways of evading authority if men care enough, and men have always cared deeply for storytelling. Perhaps if a novelist of Fielding's stature had been alive then, the play would never have flared into brief life, but the long folio romances translated from the French and Spanish must always have been a rather poor substitute for something better. So Davenant brought the play cunningly back by way of a mixed entertainment given in private—something rather like a revue with satirical dialogue and a few songs and some music.

That private atmosphere remained. When the theatres reopened—for a long while there were only two of them—the public were almost as much excluded as they had been at Davenant's entertainments. Tragedies like Dryden's *The Conquest of Granada*, written on the Corneille model in heroic couplets, with their

INTERIOR OF THE DUKE'S THEATRE, LINCOLN'S INN FIELDS
A performance of Elkannah Settle's *Empress of Morocco*, in the reign of Charles II
Engraving by Richard Sawyer

complex ideals of honour, their exaggerated unities, their exalted sentiments and complete lack of human passion, were for the educated who could judge the technical dexterity of the verse, for the enforced travellers of the Court who could appreciate the echoes of what they had heard on the Continent.

Little wonder that it was, in these court circles, a time for foreign fashions : England had given these men nothing more attractive than prison, exile, impoverishment and prudery. Tuke's blank verse romance, *The Adventure of Five Hours*, was the first great success of the new theatre — with the Court : the poor, in the theatrical eye, did not exist, and when the bourgeois began reluctantly to enter the playhouse it was to see himself mocked, for he was now of the losing party : the City had sided with Parliament, and the cuckolds and wanton city wives and leanshanked aldermen of Restoration drama represented a kind of civilised vengeance for the scaffold at Whitehall. Compare Jonson's prose comedy, *Bartholomew Fair*, with Shadwell's *Epsom Fair*, and you notice two things : a vast improvement

27

MRS. PINCHWIFE
IN WYCHERLEY'S *COUNTRY WIFE*
From Bell's *British Theatre*, 1780

in the prose and a narrowing in the scope. Jonson was writing about human nature for a public as wide as his subject : the Restoration dramatist with his infinitely more graceful instrument was fashioning an amusing bijou for the drawing-room—a witty and scandalous joke against an unpopular and rather stupid neighbour. That, of course, is to ignore Restoration tragedy, but except for a handful of plays by perhaps three authors it deserves to be ignored.

Comedy before the Restoration had been poetic, and the new comedy does on occasion reach the level of poetry. Dryden's *Marriage à la Mode*, Wycherley's *Country Wife*, Cowley's *Cutter of Coleman Street*, even " starched Johnie Crowne's " *Country Wit* and the best of Etherege build up a seacoast of Bohemia where rakes talk with the tongues of poets. You can name these plays in the same sentence as *Twelfth Night* ; the sweet sound that breathes upon a bank of violets breathes just as sweetly through the curtains of the great four-poster. And yet something has disappeared for ever : Southwark and Bankside are no longer there. *The Country Wife,* the lovely nonsense tale of the man who spread the rumour of his own impotency so that all the husbands in town left the field open to him for grazing in, is perhaps the finest prose comedy in our language. But it was not only among the dull staid citizens of the Exchange that the subtle obscenities of Mr. Horner and Lady Fidget failed to find appreciation—the rough Elizabethan mob had had another name for " china ", and something went out of our literature when society took over the theatres.

The social reign lasted roughly forty years—from the Restoration of Charles the Second to the death of Dryden, and it is dominated by that great unlovable coffee-house figure. Other men wrote single plays of greater genius, but Dryden organized his age ; he led it through the period of the heroic tragedy in couplets back to blank verse which was almost free of the Shakespearian echo, led it into the amusing parochial morass of Restoration comedy, then publicly apologised and washed his hands and led it out again towards respectability and Sheridan. And like Jonson—and unlike most of his contemporaries—he knew exactly what he was doing : his critical essays—the first example of really modern prose— blazed the way he had gone. He made the prose-play just as surely as Shakespeare made the poetic : his contemporaries may have mocked the long critical prefaces, but they accepted the standards of taste he laid down, and to a great extent we can accept them still. Aristotle dates more than Dryden. The theatre he left behind was the modern theatre even in its mechanics—the scenery, the shape of the stage. If we leave Shakespeare out of account there is no period of our dramatic literature equal to the Restoration. Pampered and artificial, appealing to the educated few, lacking in moral interest, it was yet superbly finished. Wycherley, Etherege, Aphra Behn, Sedley, even Crowne produced plays which would hold the stage now as securely as *The Importance of Being Earnest* if it were not for the conventions of modern production : these plays need

CLEOPATRA
IN DRYDEN'S *ALL FOR LOVE*
Illustration from Bell's *British Theatre*, 1780

acting in modern clothes far more than Shakespeare's : the monstrous wig, the elegant cane, the flutter of lace handkerchiefs disguise their speed and agility.

Always in the foreground is Dryden, the great Mogul : wringing poetry even out of heroic tragedy with its flattery of human nature : then contemptuously abandoning the form he had himself established to men like Elkanah Settle, the political hack who ended his days as part of the dragon at Bartholomew Fair ; planting in *Marriage à la Mode* the seed which was to flower in *The Country Wife* : already detaching himself from the obscene convention by the time Jeremy Collier launched his attack on the immorality of the stage, and in *All For Love* and *Don Sebastian* writing the last tragedies in blank verse which were to hold the stage for longer than their age. He was, as I have said, the great organizer, and the dramatic period that followed the Jacobean needed organization. It had its own darkness and its own anarchy, a flippant instead of a poetic anarchy. It is impossible to separate life and literature. Dryden almost alone among the writers of his time was ruled by an idea—the idea of authority. There is no inconsistency in his praise of Cromwell and his welcome to Charles : William he never welcomed, for by that time he had found the source of his idea and become a Catholic. Among the lechers and stoics of his time he stands as a figure of astonishing sanity : he was never taken in. One remembers the lines in *Don Sebastian* which compare the tempting stoical ideal of suicide with the Christian :—

> " But we like sentries are obliged to stand
> In starless nights and wait th' appointed hour."

The idea did not always make for perfect plays. In *The Spanish Friar*, for instance, one is aware of more thought in the background than the thin plot will stand. He produced nothing so graceful or perfect in form as Wycherley (apart from *Marriage à la Mode* most of the comedies are trivial enough, though lightened by incomparable lyrics) ; he had not the vitality in comedy of the despised Shadwell (and perhaps that was one reason for fastening a caricature of that gross figure before the eye of posterity) ; he had not perhaps—with all his logic, precision and steady growth in religious conviction—the moral genius of poor Nathaniel Lee who died in Bedlam, author of *The Princess of Cleves*, a strange Jacobean echo, but his leadership of the stage could hardly be questioned even by his enemies— who lampooned him and on one occasion set hired bravos to cudgel him as he left his coffee-house. The only man posterity has oddly enough chosen to set beside him is Otway, who, like Lee, died young and miserably. *Venice Preserved*, its blank verse written with ponderous regularity, hardly justifies his reputation. Perhaps the caricature of Shaftesbury has helped to give the play a longer life : scholars often like a little lubricity as a change from detective stories. Otway deserves to be remembered better for *The Soldier's Fortune*, a prose comedy which ranks only just below Wycherley.

Into this by no means happy company of playwrights—engaged in ferocious internecine intrigues reflected in the satires of Dryden and Rochester—Jeremy Collier was to burst with his too successful diatribe. It was as if the sense of humour had died with Charles. There followed three years of a moral stupid monarchy stiff and stubborn with the knowledge of other men's mockery, and then the Dutchman whose private life was too dubious even for lampooning was to become with his neglected queen an emblem of middle-class respectability. Dryden, Otway, Wycherley, Etherege, Shadwell, Crowne, Sedley and Behn : these in certain plays reached the height of intellectual comedy—their successors with three exceptions were only shadows. The exceptions were Vanbrugh, Farquhar and Congreve.

Vanbrugh carried on the tradition of Shadwell and Crowne—in between building those immense blocks of stone which are like the magnificent tombs of domestic greatness. His plays are on the old pattern with stupid country knights born for cuckoldry : his personal contribution was a knowledge of life which went further than the Court, the coffee-house, the New Exchange and the plays of his contemporaries—a breath of the active world and the wars in Flanders. As for Congreve, Dryden began the long tradition of overpraise. He had already

AN EIGHTEENTH CENTURY PERFORMANCE OF *HAMLET*
Oil painting by Francis Hayman, 1708-1776

handed on his laurels to several other poets before, in 1694, he wrote his lines, " To My Dear Friend, Mr. Congreve, on his Comedy called The Double Dealer " :—

> " In Him all Beauties of this Age we see ;
> Etherege his Courtship, Southern's Purity,
> The Satyre, Wit and Strength of Manly Wycherley,"

reaching the astonishing conclusion :—

> " Heav'n, that but once was Prodigal before,
> To Shakespeare gave as much ; she·cou'd not give him more."

31

The Way of the World, in which Congreve's thin and perfect talent neatly and beautifully expired " like the rose in aromatic pain," will always be the delight of the dilettante—it is the dizziest height to which an amateur author has ever climbed. Congreve, as we know from the famous meeting with Voltaire, considered himself a gentleman rather than an author ; that is why his plays remain only exquisitely worded imitations of rougher work. He contributed nothing new to the stage : the famous scene in which Millamant lays down her conditions for marriage was a polished repetition of innumerable similar scenes. Even those famous lines which describe the approach of Millamant remind us of other lines by a far greater poet—to Delilah :—

> " With all her bravery on, and tackle trim,
> Sails fill'd, and streamers waving . . ."

Poor despised Crowne, in *The Country Wit*, had provided as good situations : Shadwell had had more life, and Wycherley more stagecraft—Congreve, like the smooth schoolboy, stole the prize and remains in most people's eyes the pattern-writer of Restoration comedy.

Farquhar followed one of the fashions of his time in dying young, leaving, at the age of thirty, seven plays behind, of which *The Recruiting Officer* and *The Beaux Stratagem* are the most successful. This was the last fling of real Restoration comedy before Sentiment completely won the day, and Farquhar has a touch of genuine feeling, of wider poetry, and of the hurly-burly of experience which his predecessors lacked. *The Beaux Stratagem* is the kind of play which Fielding might have written if all his serious attention had not been given to the novel—the lovely opening in the sleepy inn with the bustle of the night coach, the unctuous innkeeper, the pretty daughter, the gentlemen of the road, and the gibbet and the horse-pistols in the background of the comedy—as if Tom Jones and Jonathan Wild had got between the same covers with the hilarity a little subdued at the approach of death (Farquhar was dying as he wrote). The satire is more human than Wycherley's, who was concerned with man only as a grotesque sexual animal, and the lyricism Etherege might have envied : above all there is a masculinity : " Give me a Man that keeps his Five Senses keen and bright as his Sword " ; the fortune hunter boasts when he pools his resources with his friend in pursuit of an heiress : " I am for venturing one of the hundreds if you will upon this Knight-Errantry ; but in case it should fail, we'll reserve the t'other to carry us to some Counterscarp, where we may die as we liv'd in a Blaze."

RICHARD BRINSLEY SHERIDAN 1751–1816
Pastel by John Russell, 1788
By courtesy of the Trustees of the National Portrait Gallery, London

OSCAR WILDE 1856–1900
Caricature by "Ape" from *Vanity Fair*, May 24th, 1884

SO long as Farquhar, Congreve and Vanbrugh lived, prose was still written for the stage with the wit and unexpectedness of poetry. When we hear of the dull-witted husband who " comes flounce into Bed, dead as a Salmon into a Fishmonger's Basket ", we are still not so far from Shakespeare and Jonson. The sense of ritual has not been lost, for ritual is the representation of something real abstracted from any individual element. It is the common touch in the human portrait—Cromwell without the personal eccentricity of the warts. Lady Fidget, it is true, is more of a " character " than Lady Macbeth, but she is still sufficiently abstracted—silly charming Wantonness itself passes across the stage as in a Morality and not a particular woman. All good dramatic prose—or poetry—has this abstract quality, by which, of course, I do not mean a wooliness, a vagueness. On the contrary the abstract word is the most concrete. But now the great period has drawn to a close. You will notice how often the writers of comedy as well as of tragedy up to now have had as their main figures representations of the dark side of human nature—Volpone, Shylock, Mr. Horner. Now sentiment is going to creep in : the author is going to fall in love with his own creations, identify himself with them, flatter himself by endowing them with all kinds of winning traits, so that we shall no longer watch Avarice, Lust, Revenge, Folly meeting the kind of fate which satisfies our sense of destiny. The happy ending is here, and we shall listen to Addison winning moral approval with the empty words of Cato, or Goldsmith's Mr. Hardcastle uttering the smug sentiments which will endear the author to his audience : " I love everything that's old : old friends, old times, old manners, old books, old wine ; and I believe, Dorothy, you'll own I have been pretty fond of an old wife ". A generation before sentiments like those could only have been uttered satirically. Now the author's personality has begun to shoulder his characters aside. We have reached the end of serious dramatic writing : only individual authors will break the general barrenness.

The high points of eighteenth century drama are usually regarded as these : *The School for Scandal*, *The Rivals*, *She Stoops to Conquer*. It must be admitted that Sheridan and Goldsmith have held the stage, if it is enough to secure year by year the compulsory attendance of school children at well-meaning matinees. The awful humours of the duel scene in *The Rivals*, Lady Teazle " m'ludding " and flirting a fan, the unconvincing villainies of Joseph Surface, the sentimentalities of Mr. Hardcastle, Mrs. Malaprop's repetitive errors—have they really delighted generations or is it only that they have been considered safe plays for young people—Restoration comedy without the sex ? Sheridan's style has the smooth unoriginal proficiency of a Parliamentary orator : Congreve lacks life but he sparkles beside his successor. There is no reason why Sheridan should have been thus preferred to such minor writers as Mrs. Centlivre—except that her humour was still a little dubious, or George Colman, whose comedy, *The Jealous Wife*,

D

THE ' SCREEN SCENE ' FROM *A SCHOOL FOR SCANDAL*
A performance at Drury Lane Theatre, May 8, 1777
Contemporary Engraving

does possess a certain tang—the atmosphere of stables and Smithfield inns : it was simply that Sheridan was a personality, and he traded himself successfully. Authors were no longer so anonymous that the researches of scholars unearth only a few bills, a doubtful signature, or an unimportant law suit.

As for Goldsmith, his success was assured as soon as the age of Nell Gwyn and Moll Davis was over. The bourgeois, who had been the butt of the theatre, ruled the stalls and boxes : respectability must be the hero now, and if a Lady Fidget were to appear at all she must be treated with solemn reprobation. Marriage is no longer the subject of a joke : it is the happy ending to which all plays tend. Typical of the period is Arthur Murphy's *The Way to Keep Him,* in which two husbands for five acts remain secretly in love with their own wives : these plays usually end with little tags—one cannot call them moral so much as conventional. " In my opinion," Murphy brings down the curtain, " were the business of this day to go abroad into the world, it would prove a very useful lesson : the men would see how their passions may carry them into the danger of wounding the bosom of a friend " (O, the shades of Mr. Horner !) " and the ladies would learn that, after the marriage rites are performed, they ought not to suffer their powers of pleasing to languish away, but should still remember to sacrifice to the Graces."

34

THEATRE IN TANKARD STREET, IPSWICH
Here Garrick made his first public appearance in 1741
Engraving, c. 1800, from Wilkinson's *Theatrum Illustrata*

It sounds more like the subject for a ladies' magazine article than a play. Compare that discreet admonitory curtain with the old comedy, with the fool singing, " For the rain it raineth every day." It was the period of blarney : Sheridan, Goldsmith, Murphy—what a lot of Irishmen from that time forth were to make a good living out of the easily pleased prosperous public of the English theatre. They all had a certain flare—Murphy could turn a phrase quite as adequately as Sheridan : here was the touch of wistful poetry—" Adieu for him the sidebox whisper, the soft assignation, and all the joys of freedom " : a certain wit—" She has touched the cash ; I can see the banknotes sparkling in her eyes," and an occasional piece of vivid and robust reporting :—

" Did not I go into Parliament to please you ? Did not I go down to the Borough of Smoke-and-Sot, and get drunk there for a whole month together ? Did not I get mobbed at the George and Vulture ? And pelted and horse-whipped the day before the election ? And was not I obliged to steal out of the town in a rabbit-cart ? And all this to be somebody as you call it ? Did not I stand up in the House to make a speech to show what an Orator you had married ? And did not I expose myself ? Did I know whether I stood upon my head or my heels for half an hour together ? And did not a great man from the Treasury Bench tell me never to speak again ? "

35

Indeed men like Murphy had a great deal of talent : they had not the dreadful melting tenderness of Goldsmith or the smoothness of Sheridan, but it is the plot now and not the theme that matters. The illustration of the idea has driven the idea itself out of the theatre. We are beginning to ask the question, " How can he get five acts out of that ? " A question which never troubled an earlier audience. It is a question which becomes increasingly troublesome the nearer we get to the persons of the play ; the less abstract the drama the more we identify ourselves with the drama. Jealousy and Passion can fill any number of acts, but the misadventures of George and Margaret cannot.

One man there was with a more robust talent, and that was Foot, the comic actor-playwright, who has been called, rather unwisely, the English Aristophanes. He cannot stand up to a term like that : racy and vigorous though his plays are, we have to use the historic sense to appreciate them, for they depend for their interest on personalities who are now buried in the footnotes of history. He did in the theatre what Rowlandson did in painting, but the paintings have outlived the plays.

The trouble was—we had been too fortunate in our drama. Not even France could boast the equal of our greatest names. With the works of Shakespeare, Jonson and Dryden to draw upon, managers found it unnecessary to encourage fresh talent. And of course it was much cheaper. Mr. W. D. Taylor has calculated that " of the thirteen parts Garrick chose to appear in during his farewell performances at the beginning of 1776, ten are from plays written before 1730," and the same critic has noted a secondary cause of decline : " The greatest geniuses of the century preferred the novel. Neither Defoe nor Richardson nor Smollett nor Sterne attempted the dramatic form." Though, in fact, Smollet did.

SCENE FROM *TWELFTH NIGHT*
Painted by William Hamilton for Boydell's 'Shakespeare Gallery'

DAVID GARRICK IN THE GREEN ROOM
Oil painting by William Hogarth, 1697-1764

THE theatre was not to see a revival until new subject-matter attracted better brains. The old abstract drama had dealt with important things : with " the base Indian who threw a pearl away richer than all his tribe," with the lark in the cage and the soul in the body ; that had gone, perhaps for ever, and the theatre had become a kind of supplement to *The Ladies' Magazine*. The religious sense was at its lowest ebb, and the political did not exist as we know it to-day. Man's interests shrank like a rockpool in the hard bright sunlight of reason. Garrick rewrote Shakespeare. (So in a small way had Davenant and Dryden, but at least they were fellow-poets : Garrick was one of the new breed of theatrical business men—the actor-managers.)

The new subject-matter therefore could not be abstract and poetic : it had to be realistic, but on a different plane of realism. It had to be important as a leading article may be important, deal with ideas important for the period if it could not deal with ideas important for all periods. Tom Robertson's *Caste*, produced in 1867, is usually held to mark the change. It is not a play which bears revival :

A PERFORMANCE OF *OTHELLO* AT THE REGENCY THEATRE, 1817
Engraving from Wilkinson's *Theatrum Illustrata*

stilted and melodramatic, it was conventional enough in everything but the one novelty, that it did state, though in primitive naïve terms, the economic and social facts : as its finest flower it was to seed the work of Pinero, Henry Arthur Jones, Galsworthy, dramatists whose plays have barely outlived their deaths.

It was the first self-seeding in the English theatre since the days of the Miracle play. Always before the seed had blown from abroad—as it was to do again at the end of the century. From Spain and France we had magnificently developed. In our own island we were shut in : there was not the intellectual room to breathe, and the absence of foreign influences in the greater part of the nineteenth century—due perhaps in part to Victorian complacency, for did not we lead the world in coal and steam and were not foreigners notoriously immoral?—had an odd and interesting effect. The theatre may sometimes appear dead, but it cannot die, and the English theatre developed in the empty years strange freaks to hold the attention. Many of these were imported from the Continent, but you can hardly dignify them by the name of influences. Our greatest actors ranted about the stage listening to imaginary bells, or mounted the scaffold as Sidney Carton—" It is a far, far better thing. . . ." It was as if a buried popular public were signalling desperately for release : as if we were on the verge of rediscovering through the crudest melodrama a popular poetry. But middle-class educated opinion was too strong.

This was the age when the producer came into his own. And the designer. Scenery had never been so important since the days of the seventeenth-century masque, but it was painfully realistic scenery. Soon we would be reading " Cigarettes by Abdullah. Vacuum cleaner in Act 2 by the Hoover Company." The Times Furnishing Company is on the horizon, and soon we would be reading of Miss So-and-so's dresses and who had made them. *Caste* had given quite a new turn to triviality.

There were attempts at better things as the century progressed—attempts which beat hopelessly against the realistic tide. There was Tennyson's *Queen Mary* and Browning's *Strafford*. But the poets were too long-winded now that they wrote to be read, and the actor-managers who produced their plays smothered their merits under the expensive costumes. Browning had a real sense of the stage. *Pippa Passes* shows what a dramatist he might have been if the audience had been there, for audiences get the dramatists they deserve (if only the critics who sneer at the bear-baiting public of Shakespeare would remember that). The quick love scene between Ottima and Sebald the first dawn after they have done away with the old doting husband is worthy of the Jacobeans—Sebald's shuddering refusal of *red* wine and Ottima's cry when conscience and despair drive them to suicide : " Not to me, God—to him be merciful." Browning, living in Italy, was free from the prudery of his age : he could afford to be honest : and his dramatic verse has the magnificent voluptuousness of a better time—" Those morbid, olive, faultless shoulder-blades." Tennyson, too, in *Queen Mary*, nearly wrote a great play. But he was hemmed in by indifference : in that prosperous and realistic age you could not deal effectively with the subtlety and the cruelty of religion. *Queen Mary* was stifled in its conception by the wordly success of the Church of England.

But these plays were as much " sports " in the Victorian theatre as Yeats's in the Edwardian, or Flecker's *Hassan*, or Eliot's *Murder in the Cathedral* in our own. The three-act play was here : the drawing-room set, the library set, and after a few more years the bedroom set. Cigarette cases were being offered, and very soon now butlers and parlour-maids would be crossing the stage, as the curtain rose, to answer the telephone. The panelling in the library looks quite Tudor, the club is lifted straight from St. James's (and now that acting has become a respectable profession the actors can be lifted from there, too).

There was something new in this : the novelty of photography—which was also to be mistaken for an art. Technically the new writers were amazingly accomplished. The theatre had become very slipshod : the soliloquy, a very valuable

By courtesy of the Trustees of the National Portrait Gallery, London

SIR ARTHUR PINERO
Oil painting by Joseph Mordecai

GEORGE BERNARD SHAW
Oil painting by Augustus John
By courtesy of the Artist and the Fitzwilliam Museum, Cambridge

convention, had become hopelessly debased, and the aside, for which there was never very much to be said, had multiplied to such an extent that almost half the play of a dramatist of Murphy's time was addressed to the audience. Pinero and Jones levelled the play up against everyday behaviour and snipped off the excrescences. Nowadays, these plays have almost an old-fashioned charm; they join Mrs. Cameron's photographs among the period pieces, but that only goes to show how up-to-the-minute they were in their own day—up-to-the-minute even in their conventionalities. The sentimentality of *London Pride* may be a little overwhelming—but so is the sentimentality of Mr. Noel Coward's *Design for Living*; we don't recognize sentimentality until it has dated a little. These writers, too, were daring: *The Second Mrs. Tanqueray*, melodramatic and sentimental though it seems now, marked an advance as great as *Caste*: sexual situations could now be presented seriously in prose if they avoided crudities likely to offend the Lord Chamberlain, just as many years later Galsworthy's *Silver Box* was to open the way to criticism of our institutions. This type of play was to reach its apotheosis in Mr. Granville-Barker's *Waste*, in which we are convincingly introduced to the private lives of Cabinet Ministers. Church disestablishment is discussed at a length that only a consummate craftsman could have made tolerable; the theme is the social convention that enforces the resignation of a Member of Parliament who is co-respondent in a divorce suit: the title of course refers to the waste involved in the retirement of the one Minister capable of nursing through Parliament the Disestablishment Bill. Mr. Barker might have written a play about Parnell, but he chose deliberately the rather drab political issue, just as Henry James in his later novels chose ugly names for his heroines: above all there must be no fortuitous glamour to confuse the subject with the plot. No other play of the realistic school is so likely to survive the circumstances of its time. It is honest through and through, and it is without a trace of the sentimentality that betrayed Galsworthy.

There was, of course, bound sooner or later to be a reaction against this sober high-minded pattern. Dryden, it was said, found English prose brick and left it marble: these authors were certainly remaking it in rather ugly bricks like a workhouse wall. One bright spirit had evaded capture, leaving behind him, after he had died of drink and disease, one of the most perfect plays in our theatre. How beautifully free from any sense of period at all is Wilde's *Importance of Being Earnest*. In *Lady Windermere's Fan* he tried to play the game like his contemporaries, but he had not their sense of reality and the result was rather like an Academy problem picture, but in *The Importance* he shook off his age and soared as freely in the delirious air of nonsense as Edward Lear.

Meanwhile, with critics like Mr. Bernard Shaw and William Archer in the stalls, a certain depression over the North Sea was bound to strike our shores. Henry James mercilessly described the atmosphere of Ibsen's plays as " an odour of spiritual paraffin"; the long Oslo winter and the light of oil lamps had helped to form these extraordinary plays in which town councillors and sanitary inspectors wrestled with their egos as ferociously as the Prince of Denmark in surroundings of appalling drabness. To audiences accustomed to Pinero these plays were inexpressibly odd and obscure : factions developed, with critics in opposing camps : the cause was not helped by Archer's creaking translations. *The Doll's House* had a comparatively easy passage : ' women's rights ' was a subject even Pinero might have tackled, but *The Master Builder, The Wild Duck* — this mixture of poetic symbolism and realistic detail could not be understood by that generation. It was as strange to Shakespeare lovers as to Pinero " fans." And before they had really time to accept Ibsen a second northern depression reached our island, this time from Russia ; and the Stage Society produced Tchekhov.

But Pinero, Jones and, increasingly, Galsworthy, and later Maugham, remained the staple fare, though perhaps the general shaking-up by Ibsen and Tchekhov caused as near an approach to passionate approval and fanatical disapproval as the English public could express, and helped the success of two authors who stood right outside the realistic social convention — Shaw and Barrie. Ibsen had introduced intellectual discussion to the stage, and Shaw seized his opportunity ; though perhaps it is too fantastic to detect a resemblance between the frustrated hopes, the wistful dreams and the strangely natural behaviour of Tchekhov's characters and Barrie's fairy backgrounds, enchanted woods, and Never Neverlands.

It would be idle here to attempt to scratch the tough surface of Mr. Shaw's enormous world-wide reputation. With Wilde, Byron, Galsworthy and Edgar Wallace he is the representative of our literature on the Continent. Like Sterne, another Irishman, he plays the fool at enormous length, but without that little bitter core which lies hidden in *Tristram Shandy*. Ideas are often adopted for the sake of their paradoxes and discarded as soon as they cease to startle. He gives his audiences a sense of intellectual activity — but they often imagine they have exercised their brains when they have really done no more than strain their eyes at the startling convolutions of a tumbler.

Barrie was as ill at ease in the world as Shaw is confident. Favoured from the very start of his career by Fortune he remained a misfit. He invented a dream world of sexless wives who mothered and understood their husbands, of children who never grew up because they had never really been born. His plays are cloyingly sweet, but there had been no dramatic writer since the seventeenth century who knew his business so well. The opening act of *Dear Brutus* for example could not be bettered : from the opening line as the ladies drift in after dinner he holds you with his Ancient Mariner's eye. He wrote with ease and grace and he was a consummate craftsman : " Had you with these the same but brought a mind." But yet when all is said, he *had* enlarged the subject matter

ARTHUR CECIL AS MR. POSKETT IN PINERO'S *THE MAGISTRATE*
Water colour by Graham Robertson

of our drama : he had improved its prose style : yet it is odd that his plays should have led nowhere. . . .

One great dramatist was working in our century : one pictures him reading Flaubert in Paris, walking the boulevards to keep warm and save coal, learning the kind of seriousness which the French can teach better than any other nation : the intense seriousness of finding the right word and the right method whether you are writing farce or tragedy. This is the seriousness you do not find in Shaw or Barrie or Galsworthy—from whom pity for an unrealized lower-class drove

43

J. M. BARRIE
Drawing by W. T. Monnington, 1932

out every consideration of style or form. But Synge exchanging the boulevards for the West Coast of Ireland, lying flat on the bedroom floor of his inn with his ear to a crack, recording the phrases of the peasantry with scrupulous accuracy, was as careful and serious an artist as Flaubert. He reminds one of " the chief inquisitor " in Browning's poem :—

> " He took such cognisance of men and things,
> If any beat a horse you felt he saw ;
> If any cursed a woman he took note ;
> Yet stared at nobody—they stared at him."

The Shadow in the Glen, The Riders to the Sea : these were the exquisite marginal drawings for the two great compositions, *The Well of the Saints* and

The Playboy of the Western World. The last play caused a riot in the Dublin theatre where it was first presented—but no riot was ever caused in London. The excessive tolerance of that city (often amounting to indifference) allows it to accept everything without protest. Indifference can almost have the air of charity; but you cannot live on indifference, and Synge had not the secret of his fellow Irishman to shake London audiences into attention—he would not have wanted the secret. His work was done for the work's sake; personality was something to be excluded at all costs. The only hostility he aroused was in such places as the *Punch* office: a few comic writers wrote little sneering parodies of the Irish manner as they had written little sneering parodies of the Russian manner. Parodies sometimes have effects their authors never dreamed of, and I remember that my own first introduction to Synge was a parody in *Punch* when I was about fourteen years old—I went about for days with the magic of the silly jest in my ears.

Synge died young, and again there was no successor; even in Ireland every new playwright had to begin over again and conquer the enmity of the Irish people.

IN this short survey we have reached our own times, and it is a little invidious to hand out bouquets and poisoned chalices to contemporaries. But it is impossible not to notice the dead end. There are fine plays, but no single figure dominates and directs his age as Dryden and Jonson did. One cannot say the poetic drama shows no sign of life, when one has seen the success of *Murder in the Cathedral*. Somerset Maugham in *Our Betters* wrote perhaps the best social comedy of this century, and in *The Sacred Flame* he certainly wrote one of the worst dramas. Ronald Mackenzie in *Musical Chairs* made a magnificent beginning under Tchekhov's influence and was then killed in a motor accident. J. B. Priestley has tried to enlarge the contemporary subject matter with the help of Dunne, and you cannot say experiment is quite dead so long as Sean O'Casey and Denis Johnstone are writing. As for craftsmanship, Noel Coward has all his contemporaries beaten. He is the best craftsman since Barrie and unlike Barrie is able to disguise his sentimentality, coming into the open only occasionally in such pieces as *Cavalcade*. Only as the years pass and the contemporary idiom changes does his sentimentality begin to show, emerging as the dye washes off, like the colour of a stolen horse. One other dramatist I should like to include here, and that is Vernon Sylvaine, the author of *Women Aren't Angels* and other farces designed for the Robertson Hare, Alfred Drayton combination. These plays with their great technical skill and their very national humour—full of discarded trousers and men dressed up in their wives' clothes and jealous women and timid husbands —are much more serious in the aesthetic sense than such fake tragedies as *The Sacred Flame* and *Loyalties*, which are exclusively written for the stalls and the upper circle.

It is a " bitty " picture, the contemporary theatre—so many talented authors, so many plays of great competence and even of some seriousness, and yet surrounding every effort this sense of a huge public indifference. In that lies the chief distinction between the English and the American theatre : over here we write perhaps just as many good plays, but in New York they have a good audience. There is in the air an interest, an excitement—at any moment, you feel, the great dramatist may appear again because the audience is ready to receive him.

The economics of the London theatre have a great deal to do with this indifference : the huge theatre rents make managers unwilling to take risks, and like cinema companies they stick to the familiar pattern of entertainment (it is the small theatres—the Westminster, the Mercury, the Duchess and the Unity— which have been responsible for most of the experiments we have seen of late years). The rents, too, raise the price of seats, so that theatre-going becomes the privilege of an economic class and of middle age. The young and the poor may squeeze into the gallery, but the " Gods " are powerless to influence the entertainment far below them.

J. M. SYNGE
Wash drawing by J. B. Yeats

But the picture is not wholly dark: the "Old Vic" has kept Shakespeare before the people, the small theatres are there, and it is unlikely that the high rental of the west end will survive the war. The indifference of London to living art has been the indifference of a class, of the well-to-do and the professional man cut to pattern by his education. The theatre is bound up with the world's fate as it has always been: young, lyrical, conceited in the first Elizabethan theatre: dark with disillusionment and violence in the Jacobean; clever and conscienceless and making hay while the sun shone in the interval between two revolutions; moribund, living on the imagination of the past during the age of reason; journalistic and humanitarian during the reign of Victoria; confused and indecisive in our own times. . . . Now we are heading either for chaos of such long duration that the theatre will not survive our civilization, or a world so new and changed it may well be that in the theatre it will seem as though Elizabeth were on the throne again.

DESIGN FOR *A WINTER'S TALE*
Drawing by Albert Rutherston, 1928